AUBREY BEARDSLEY

REJANE

AUBREY BEARDSLEY

SIXTY SELECTED DRAWINGS

academy editions · london
St. Martin's Press · New York

First published in 1967
Reprinted 1969, 1970
Revised edition 1970
Reprinted 1972 (twice)

First published in Great Britain by Academy Editions,
7 Holland Street, London W.8.
©1967, 1972 by Academy Editions. All rights reserved.

First published in the United States of America in 1972 by
St. Martin's Press Inc., 175 Fifth Avenue, New York, N.Y. 10010
Affiliated publishers: Macmillan Company Limited, London -
also at Bombay, Calcutta, Madras and Melbourne -
The Macmillan Company of Canada Limited, Toronto.

Library of Congress Catalog Number 78-18583.

Printed in Great Britain by The Pitman Press, Bath.

INTRODUCTION

In 1898, Aubrey Beardsley died, aged twenty-five. He came from a background of genteel poverty and started his working life in a surveyor's office. Yet within five years he had created a taste and given his name to a period. With minimal formal art training, he produced some of the most original, disturbing and exquisite line drawings of any English artist.

He achieved fame, or rather notoriety, astonishingly quickly. His first chance - commissioned illustrations, the *Morte d'Arthur* cycle, although sometimes confused and burdened with decorative and derivative detail - demonstrated his masterly linear virtuosity and the curious world of his concentrated and intensely personal imagination. As a result, he was chosen to illustrate Wilde's *Salomé* in 1894. That the illustrations are often irrelevant to the text and irreverent to the author established his attitude as an illustrator and his relationship to most of the literary artistic "underworld" personalities with whom he was associated.

The *Salomé* drawings shocked and excited contemporaries. There was no precedent in English nineteenth century graphic art for his deployment of a single line in conjunction with masses of black, for the absence of the accepted norms of descriptive representation and the pictorial resolution of dramatic tension in such stark terms of space, outline and mass. The distinctive and provocative style, allied to a pervasive eroticism (not merely implicit but explicit by contemporary standards) led to his appointment as art-editor of the self-consciously avant-garde *Yellow Book* at twenty-three. Also to his public identification with impropriety and lubricity - prompting a reviewer to recommend that a short Act of Parliament should be passed "to stop this sort of thing".

"This sort of thing" is the quality which makes Beardsley's work instantly recognisable despite important stylistic changes. Whilst his linear convolutions, the decorative treatment of both form and substance as a two-dimensional pattern and even the conventionalised content of much of his work became the staple of *Art Nouveau,* the "jealous intensity" of his emotional and artistic vision effectively distinguished his large output from that of his many imitators.

Tuberculosis, diagnosed as a child, which killed him as a young man, forced him to become a detached spectator whose imagination was fed more by literary than personal contact. The heightened sexuality associated with the disease became in his case an indiscriminate imaginative eroticism, cruel, grotesque and evocative, having its roots in mental excitation deprived of physical fulfilment. Incest, homosexuality, diabolism, phallusanbetung were attributed to him but the tragic betrayal of his urgent desires by a diseased body is exemplified in the foetus-headed monsters, subtly debauched maidens, hermaphrodite youths and grimly-questing women haunting his work in a graphic extension of emotional fantasy. Yet to focus only on this aspect of his work is to repeat the crass judgement of his philistine contemporaries. His (very) dirty book *Under The Hill* is a lighthearted satire on the gamut of sexual permutations and his theatrical and musical illustrations, endlessly inventive costumes, carefully observed social sketches and witty caricatures warn us not to judge his achievements by his sexual preoccupation.

During the first Wilde trial the offices of the *Yellow Book* were attacked and Beardsley dismissed, as a scapegoat to the public fit of moral indignation. He was left in rapidly deteriorating health, with no regular source of income, increasingly dependent on his beloved mother and sister and financially maintained by the dubious Smithers and questionable Raffilovich. From this period date the decorative *Savoy* drawings and the equivocal *Lysistrata* cycle, denounced as obscene by the artist on his convert's death-bed. In these, flat pen and ink lines are employed to the exclusion of intermediate tones, recession or background in a concentrated economy of uncompromising decorative austerity.

To contrast the *Lysistrata* drawings with the passionately detailed rococo illustrations to *The Rape of the Lock* makes patent the limitation of his popular reputation. These are a supreme example of pictorial commentary on a literary text in which form and content are controlled by a rigorous intellectual and artistic discipline. Beerbohm said that "no man ever saw more than Beardsley" and his validity as an artist, not merely as a quintessentially chic and superably dextrous ornamentalist, lies in his ability to draw the spectator into a voyeuristic alliance, sharing the totality of the artist's grotesque, ironic and tragic private world.

THE PLATES

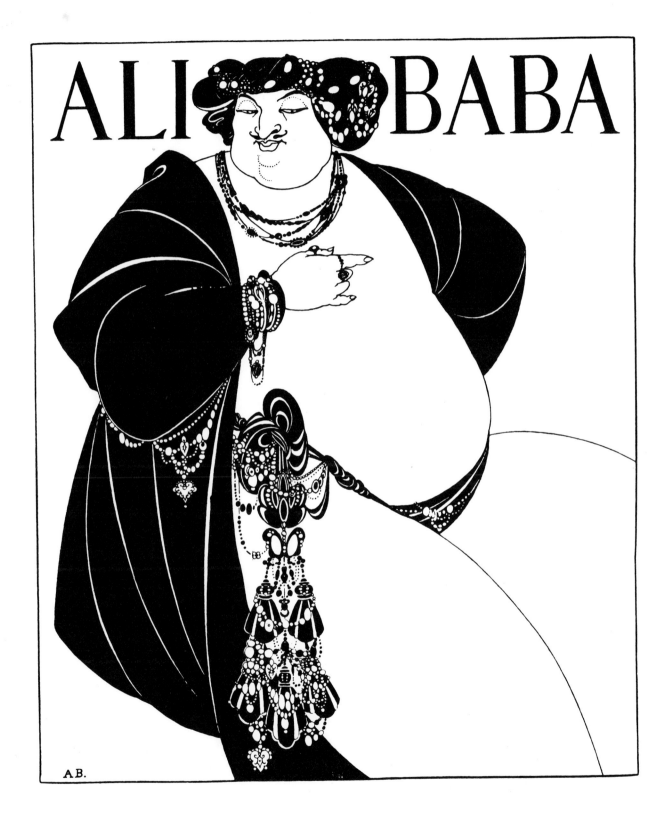

LYSISTRATA.

AVBREY
BEARDSLEY

13

AUBREY BEARDSLEY, ETC.

30

THE
SAVOY

AVBREY
BEARDSLEY

AVBREY BEARDSLEY. 1895

40

MESSALINA.

AUBREY BEARDSLEY

THE SCARLET
PASTORALE

VENUS.

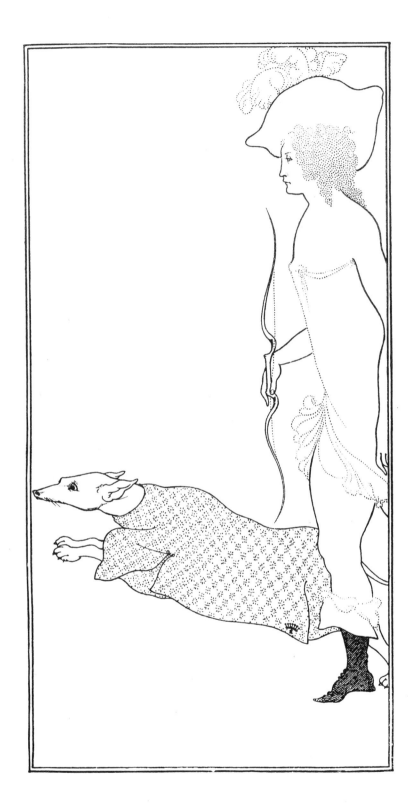

AUBREY BEARDSLEY.